"Max's life story is an inspirational tale proving grit and determination matter more than educational pedigree or celebrity connections."

—**John Warrillow**
Founder, The Value Builder System
Author of *Built to Sell* and *The Automatic Customer*

"Max Mabuti's story is inspiring and heart-warming. He has risen from humble beginnings and against adversity to a place of prominence in the business world in South Africa, achieving international recognition along the way. Using his knowledge of and passion for boxing as his guiding framework, he's proven to be an absolute champion as an entrepreneurial businessman. More importantly, he's shown himself to be an outstanding humanitarian, one who has unselfishly shared his self-gained understanding, insight, and success with others so that they, too, may have the opportunity to accomplish what he has done."

—**Dr. T. A. Marsh**
Retired Former Campus Director at Rhodes University,
East London Campus

"So much has been written about the complexity of the South African situation and the challenges faced by, particularly, black people during apartheid. This discourse is valid and needs to be documented, as we must always learn from the past. Equally, if not more important for the future of the country, is to document the experiences that successful black entrepreneurs have had as they've realized their dreams. Max Mabuti is such an individual. He's a grounded visionary, and it's been my privilege to know and mentor him in various guises for almost a decade. It takes courage to document a story such as Max has done, and I hope that readers learn and grow from it."

—Dr. Wanda Chunnett
Director, Turner and Townsend

"As a business coach, some of the crucial qualities I look for in entrepreneurs are their level of engagement, tenacity, and coachability. When I met Max Mabuti in 2017, I quickly realised he has bucketloads of these characteristics and plenty more.

The story of his first order of air conditioners for Flat Foot struck me as being absolutely typical of the entrepreneurial mindset needed to succeed in a demanding environment. Max is one of the very few entrepreneurs who can hustle, not allowing anything to stand in his way to achieve his goals. This attitude was clearly birthed in his days as a professional boxer. Your journey so far is just the beginning, Max!"

—Cameron Burt
Mentor and Business Coach-
Director Marketdoor Solution

"Max gives a one-two punch to the trials and tribulations of coming from behind to become a successful business entrepreneur. I've had the pleasure of meeting Max personally, and this book is an inspiring story of success after starting from nothing. There's much to be learned about faith, perseverance, and true grit. This inspiring story will make you want to endure and do more."

—Terry Lammers, CVA
Managing Member, Innovative Business Advisors, LLC
Author of *You Don't Know What You Don't Know*

"Contrary to our white counterparts in business who mostly inherit generational wealth—not just in financial terms but also in valuable, practical business training from a young age—black entrepreneurs go through a lot of trial and error with an abundance of painful lessons learnt through failure.

All that pain became the fertilizer that nurtured an organic business achiever who refused to bow down to the myriad of obstacles on the path towards success.

Nobody espouses this reality more than Max. The Flat Foot story is one of resilience, of the grit-your-teeth-and-push-forward philosophy in a way that inspires those who are still going through the ups and downs of business to keep their chins up and strive on.

Not only will aspiring business people gain insight into the real, practical world of business, but the life lessons in the book are applicable to all facets of life.

An inspirational read indeed."

—Ace Ncobo
World renowned former professional soccer referee,
Serial Entrepreneur, Business Leader and Coach,
CEO of Black Business Forum

THE FLAT
FOOT STORY

THE FLAT FOOT STORY

FROM PROFESSIONAL BOXER
TO BUILDING A BUSINESS

A South African Entrepreneurial Journey

MAX MABUTI

Stonebrook Publishing
Saint Louis, Missouri

A STONEBROOK PUBLISHING BOOK

This book was guided in development and
edited by Nancy L. Erickson, The Book Professor®
TheBookProfessor.com

Library of Congress Control Number: 2022902723

ISBN: 978-1-955711-11-1

www.stonebrookpublishing.net

PRINTED IN THE UNITED STATES OF AMERICA

For my family:

My wife Vanessa; my children;

my two sisters, Thantaswa and Buyiswa;

my brother Timoti; my mother, Dudu;

and last, but not least, my late father, Wellington.

CONTENTS

INTRODUCTION

Flat Foot Engineering is an ISO 9001:2015 company with a staff of seventy, comprised of a strong technical team of over forty technical field personnel and an administrative support and finance team led by a solid, well-structured management team that has a wealth of experience in engineering and facilities management. We are headquartered in East London, South Africa, with branches in Port Elizabeth, Mthatha (a small "city" in the Eastern Cape with an estimated population of about 78,000 people), and a growing presence in Johannesburg. We are on a drive to achieve a national footprint.

We are one of the biggest service providers for the Eastern Cape Department of Health for electro-mechanical maintenance, servicing three hundred medical facilities in the province, including full-time maintenance and operations of coal-fired boilers at government hospitals. We have executed several boiler and steam lines repairs, including yearly to three-yearly boiler services on various boiler sizes.

In addition to boilers and steam lines, our services also include installation, repairs, and maintenance of sterilising equipment (autoclaves), kitchen and laundry equipment, heating, ventilation, air conditioning (HVAC), and refrigeration. We also manufacture hot water pressure vessels at a small scale in our Port Elizabeth workshop. We're hoping to grow this division to manufacture at a large scale. At one point, we supplied coal to all the public hospitals in the Eastern Cape. Amongst our other key customers are Pragma (an enterprise asset management engineering company), local and district municipalities, Sun International, Barclays, the Department of Public Works, Sundale Dairy, Eskom, and the Coega Development Corporation (CDC).

Flat Foot is a Level-1 BEE (Broad-based Black Economic Empowerment) contributor, meaning that our ownership is 100 percent black, and we have a Construction Industry Development Board (CIDB) grading of 6ME PE. The CIDB is a South African government entity that regulates the construction industry and grades companies according to their ability and capacity, with a grading range from one to nine.

We turned over $2.3 million (+/- ZAR 32 million) in the previous financial year and are on track to turn over a minimum of approximately $3.4 million (+/- ZAR 47 million) in the current financial year. We are a member of the Top 40 National Gazelles under the banner of the Department of Small Business Development (DSBD). The National Gazelles is an initiative of the DSBD and the Small Enterprise Development Agency (SEDA), which was launched in 2015 as a programme aimed at propelling the top forty selected high-growth small and medium enterprises (SMEs) in South Africa to the next level through multiple support provisions and interventions. The SMEs that have been in business for two years or more, employ two or more people, and turn over ZAR one million per annum qualify to apply to be part of the programme.

We are a strong supporter of small, previously disadvantaged business development, and we share business opportunities with small up-and-coming businesses owned by previously disadvantaged individuals, aiming to help them sustain their growth.

Flat Foot was awarded the ROCCI/FNB Business of the Year Award in 2017 in the Engineering category, selected as the SEDA Ambassador in 2017, and awarded the Oliver Top Empowerment Award in 2018. We are the appointed dealers for Samsung, Daikin, and (Carrier) Metraclark. As part of our commitment to playing a positive role in the communities in which we operate, we are affiliated with the non-profit organisation Community Organization Guardians of Hope, whose focus is to take care of abandon babies and give them a second chance in life. Our business has been featured in several magazines, case studies, and even research projects by the World Bank as one of the top entrepreneurial businesses in South Africa and a contributor to the government's National Development Plan.

Together with Community Action Africa and the University of Fort Hare, we also sponsor the Annual Youth Debate that takes place at the University of Fort Hare in East London.

This is our story.

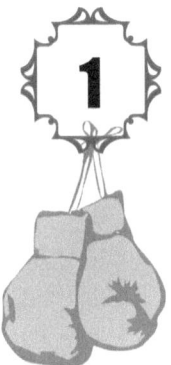

AN ABJECT BEGINNING

I was born in a small town in what used to be called the Republic of Transkei. Back then, it was an unrecognized state in the southeastern region of South Africa. We were a family of six children: my three sisters, my two brothers, and me. My father was a reverend who ministered to farms around East London on the southeast coast that bordered the Indian Ocean. We lived in a mission house on a farm in Silverdale, about twenty-four kilometres from East London, which was surrounded by forests and isolated from the public.

In 1980, when I was about five years old, I remember my mother giving me a hard slap on my head.

"Why are you talking about that terrorist?" she asked. "Do you want us to get arrested?"

I was stunned. What had I done wrong? I had only said, "Viva Mandela!" as I imitated two men who had walked past the farm in their camouflage uniforms. At that age, I knew nothing about politics, but I later learned that these men were the liberation soldiers of Umkhonto we Sizwe, the military wing of the African National Congress that was founded by Nelson Mandela. Their mission was to fight against the South African government to gain greater rights for black people like us. That's why they were considered a terrorist organization; apartheid had not yet realized its death. No wonder my mother was afraid.

My grandmother, Nina Boetie, as we called her, was my best friend. She was everything to me, but I thought it strange that she couldn't communicate with my mother, her own daughter. They didn't speak the same language. Nina Boetie spoke Afrikaans. My mother had also spoken that language at one time, but when she was twelve years old, she was sent to the Republic of Transkei to live with her father's family. Her father believed that if she grew up in Cape Town, where they lived, she would learn bad habits, so he sent my mother and her two sisters to their grandparents' home in Transkei.

In Transkei, the people spoke fluent Xhosa, not Afrikaans, so my mother forgot how to speak her native language. In 1979, she reunited with her mother and father, and we all lived in the huge farmhouse together.

One Friday afternoon, my brother and I were waiting outside for our father to return home from East London. My little sister, Thantaswa, was still a baby at the time. Finally, our grandmother called to us as the sun was setting.

"Mabhisi!" she shouted; she could not pronounce my older brother's name, which was Mcebisi.

"*Kom hier na toe, is laat nou, kom binne by die huis,*" she said in Afrikaans. "Come here, it's late. Come inside the house."

We quietly went back inside, disappointed that we couldn't wait at the gate for our father. When he eventually returned, it was late. He came to our room as usual and gave us some treats, which we gobbled up right away. Around 9:00 p.m., we all went to bed and fell asleep.

About an hour later, we heard a big crash from the window in the dining room. My father woke up and shouted, "What is that?" He got up to look around. "Who is there?" he asked in a low voice.

My father was a very fit fellow who was well-practised in karate, so we all felt protected. But within seconds, he was flat on the floor, knocked down by a brick that had been hurled through the window and hit him in the back of his head.

My mother came flying out of the bedroom to try to protect my father, but five black men were already inside the house. Taking stock of the situation, she quickly pushed all five of us children underneath our bed and told us to hide.

We watched and listened while they beat my mother and my father so badly that I thought they were dead. My seventy-year-old grandfather also tried to fight the brutes, but he was frail, and there was nothing much he could do. Mocking him, one of the monsters raised a baseball bat, aimed at my grandfather's head, and swung hard to crush his skull.

With my mother and father lying in a pool of blood and my grandfather left on the floor to die, the unscrupulous animals took everything in our house—including my older sister Gladys. She wasn't gone long. They raped her, then brought her back to us.

Finally, my mother regained consciousness. I'll never know how she survived the gash in her head from being beaten with an axe. Wounded as she was, she somehow managed to get up and walk approximately ten kilometres to get help.

Because we lived so far away from other people, it took a long time for help to arrive. Four hours later, the police and ambulances arrived. My grandfather was declared dead at the scene, and they took my mother, father, and sister to a public hospital in East London. My father was so badly hurt that they had to install a metal plate in his head. While in the hospital, they discovered that my mother was pregnant with my little brother Timothy. It was a miracle that she didn't miscarry.

After that, life was never the same for us—certainly not for me. I was tortured by venomous anger towards these criminals, and I wanted revenge.

* * *

In 1983, my father decided to relocate us to a village called Nxaruni, East London. That's where I started my primary education. I was a hot-headed, angry child, and I knew I needed to find a way to redirect my anger. So, I started going to a boxing gym to train to become a boxer. I wasn't too happy to discover that the first thing I'd have to learn in boxing was discipline rather than beating people.

One Monday afternoon, tired from school, my hand trembled as I reached for the doorknob. It was locked. My trainer had warned me not to arrive late at the gym. He never wanted us to miss any part of his teachings and training. Yes, that day I was late, and I knew I was wrong, but nevertheless, I decided to go anyway because I was a disciplined boxer.

"You are late," he said as I entered the building, "but it's better to be late than never." For my transgression, my trainer ordered me to do ten press-ups as punishment.

Boxing framed my life, and my boxing training continues to play a profound role in my life. In boxing, discipline is key. You must respect your trainer, you have to respect your clubmates, and, perhaps most importantly, you have to respect your body. It was good to learn this early in life, and it came in very handy later in business, as I respected my mentor, I respected my team, and I respected my business. What I learned in boxing became my framework for life.

After losing my grandfather in the brutal attack, my grandmother was exceedingly lonely, and she decided to go back home to where she was born. She lived there for a few years with her sister and eventually passed on. I, on the other hand, became a boxer because I wanted to learn survival skills and how to beat people—not only physically but also psychologically.

※ ※ ※

Early on a Friday morning in 1994, the day I was writing my final matric paper at my respected school, I heard a knock on my door.

"Who is it?" I asked, exhausted from studying late the previous night. It was my father. He'd brought me some water to wash myself for school, knowing that I would soon be writing my last exam.

"Here, take the water to bathe yourself," he said. "I woke up early this morning to prepare it for you."

"Thank you, Father," I responded with a smile, grateful for the time he'd saved me.

"Remember, life is about helping others," he said.

I appreciated this gift. In our rural area, we had no electricity and no indoor bathrooms or toilets. To prepare warm water to bathe in, you had to go outside and make a fire. Then you had to fetch the water, pour it into the big pot we had for just this purpose, and wait until it was warm. Only then could you pour the water into the basin to wash yourself. My father had gotten up early to do all of that for me.

After we finished writing our last exam, my friends and I went out to barbeque some meat in celebration. We stayed out with some other friends until 9:00 p.m. when I decided to go home. It was pitch black outside; the villages had no streetlights. Whilst walking in the dark, I saw my little brother Timothy running toward me.

"What's wrong?" I asked him.

"It's our father," he answered, crying.

I didn't ask any questions and ran straight to the house, where I found my mother crying. Quietly, I went to the bedroom. My father was lying stone-still in his bed. I took one look at him and knew he had passed. I closed his eyes and broke down in grief-stricken sobs. I couldn't believe he was gone. The man I looked up to was no more.

Now I had to be strong for my family and plan my future.

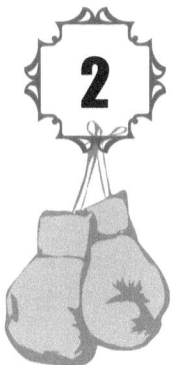

SEIZING OPPORTUNITY

After the funeral a few days later, I felt the full force of my responsibility for my family, even though I was still in school. I didn't know what direction to take, so I started looking for a short-term job. I was soon hired as a truck loader at an alcohol distribution company for the December holidays.

When the matric exam results were announced in January, I discovered I'd done very well—well enough to get a matric exemption, which meant I could get into any South African university. What's more, our school was in the top ten schools in South Africa in terms of the matric examination pass rate. That credential prompted the Minister of Education, Sibusiso Bengu, to visit our school and commit to building us a new school, a promise he fulfilled. Ngwenyathi Senior Secondary School now boasts a new building because of our hard work and academic success.

When I saw my test results, I decided to go to university and secure the necessary sponsorship I'd need for the tuition. Luckily, our community was in partnership with the Kellogg Foundation, which wanted to sponsor the top achievers in the Newlands community and award them with a full bursary (scholarship) to study at a university. Because I was one of the top achievers in my school, I was awarded a bursary to study full time at Rhodes University at their campus in East London.

When I arrived at Rhodes in 1995, it was just after our first democratic elections that had been held in April of 1994. For the first time, all South Africans—black and white—were allowed to vote for the government of our choice. The Government of National Unity was formed, and Nelson Mandela was elected as president of South Africa.

With the changes in equality so recent, there were still very few black students at the university. Furthermore, I had come from the former Bantu education system, a vastly inferior race-based education, which couldn't compare to the education the whites had received. It was my first time studying at a multi-racial establishment.

At that time, Rhodes had two campuses: the main campus in Grahamstown and the satellite campus in East London, which I attended. Because of the two geographical locations, we were allowed to have two Student Representative Council (SRC) presidents, one from East London and one from Grahamstown. In 1997, I was elected unopposed as the SRC president in East London, having been involved in student politics since 1996 (my second year at university) through the ANC student move-ment SASCO (South African Student Congress). Chico Khoza was elected as the president in Grahamstown (another SASCO member). I was also elected as a member of the university sen-ate. This was when I discovered I had leadership potential.

As students in those days—and still quite exhilarated by our newfound democratic freedom—we agreed to form a united student body for all the universities in South Africa. A unified structure was launched, and I was elected as the Secretary General of South African universities' SRCs, a body that investigated the issues affecting all the universities in South Africa. I worked very closely with the president of the Walter Sisulu University (WSU), the famous Advocate Thembela Ngcukaitobi (who represented the Economic Freedom Fighters (EFF) in their court case against President Zuma regarding the Nkandla scandal), and the current commissioner of South Africa's Competition Commission, Tembinkosi Bonakele, who was the SRC president at Fort Hare at the time.

After graduating with honours in development studies, I was employed by Sektor Engineering, which appointed me to head the land restitution process of the East Bank and West Bank communities in East London. This was for the families who had been removed by the apartheid government from the eastern and western banks of the Buffalo River to Duncan Village and Mdantsane, respectively.

After a year and a half, I got a job with Coca-Cola® in East London as a sales representative. I was given a job with no customers, so I had to create a new route for myself! Within one week, I had gained twenty new customers. The management couldn't believe what I had achieved. My strategy was very simple. I went to the ignored market, the shebeens and the spaza shops, the unofficial or informal shops in the townships. No one had ever approached them before, and they were happy to sign on with me.

I worked for Coca-Cola® for two years and then took another opportunity to be a field marketing executive with a company that was contracted by Vodacom. My job was to grow the former Transkei market for the company to thwart a new player that was entering the field—MTN, a new cell phone service provider.

My territory included Mthatha; I call it the mini-Johannesburg. I learned a great deal here, including how to be a hustler and how to survive with no money. On this teaching ground, I realised my entrepreneurial potential, and more importantly, I believed in myself. I thought I could do anything, and I was right.

Things were exciting in my business life, but tragedy struck at home. My older sister Gladys passed away. Then my brother, Mcebisi, committed suicide by throwing himself off a mountain in Nxaruni. This was my brother who had been so proud of me. He called me *bhulu leplasi*, which meant "white farmer," a nickname he gave me because I was light complected and liked to wear shorts like a farmer.

Losing two children was an enormous blow to my mother. My mother, as strong as she was, was distraught with grief. I vowed to do everything in my power to support my mother financially and emotionally. I would always take care of her.

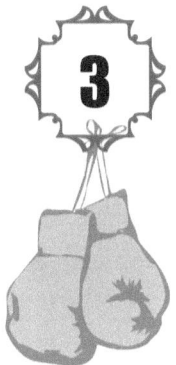

THE ENTREPRENEURIAL SEED

I drove my Alaska-blue Toyota Corolla from East London to look for a place to live. My plan was to work from home. My immediate line manager was in Johannesburg. Arriving in Mthatha, I drove along the very busy Madeira Street, where I parked next to the local Kentucky Fried Chicken to buy some lunch. As I was getting out of my car, I saw a red Toyota van down the road but thought nothing of it until I heard a loud crash as it smashed into my car from behind. Then it took off!

What a welcome to Mthatha! Fortunately, there was a police station on Madeira Street, and within five minutes, the police arrived and took my statement.

This rather negative initial experience notwithstanding, life was enjoyable and exciting. At thirty-one years old, full of energy and enthusiasm, my life was good.

When I first started working in Mthatha, the idea of starting Flat Foot had not yet been born. As a field marketer, I was responsible for the former homeland of Transkei[1], and my job was to create awareness about Vodacom's products in the Eastern Cape. I enjoyed my work, and it gave me an opportunity to travel and experience more of my country and its people.

I was inspired by local entrepreneurs who were going the distance and building successful small businesses. I observed a gap in the market where black people were less represented in the trade. Mechanical engineering was largely dominated by white people; less than 10 percent were black. And the government called for black entrepreneurs to step forward and help employ our generation of people—to contribute to the rainbow nation. I wanted to create a business that would come into this sector, build a legacy, and establish a business that could operate independently of me in the future. If others could do it, so could I.

I began doing some research about starting a business and learning from the Transkei people. I found that running a business is not child's play. You need the stamina to go the distance and to press on, especially when things are not going your way. It also requires believing in yourself and your product or service.

Eventually, I was fired from my job. My focus on my personal research had impacted my work. I do not blame them for dismissing me, as I would have done the same if I had been the manager of IDSC, the company contracted by Vodacom for field marketing.

I now had enough time on my hands to pursue my business venture. With no money and just a dream, I joined and started several companies consulting for government projects.

---

[1] During the apartheid regime in South Africa, black people were allocated to the so-called homelands. These homelands were divided in the TBVC states of Transkei, Bophuthatswana, Venda, and Ciskei. After democracy, these states were dissolved and reunited back into South Africa.

Some of these companies were ultimately liquidated, and some I resigned from to start Flat Foot Engineering. In 2003, I joined a company called Adisa Consultants. We had so many challenges to contend with, the biggest of which was cash flow. We ended up opting for voluntary liquidation because we could not sustain the business.

At one point, my friends, Mfumba and Sparks, and I joined a business in Port Nolloth, where we also worked with a community organisation to mine the diamond dumps at one of Alexkor's mines in the Northern Cape. I personally went there to mine diamonds, but unfortunately, we ended up losing money due to our outdated technology. We could not afford the latest technology, and we eventually abandoned the mine.

Running a business is not for the faint-hearted—you need courage to succeed.

※ ※ ※

I had always wanted to start a unique business, something that could grow and become a major player in its industry. In 2005, I registered an air-conditioning business, Flat Foot Engineering, that specialized in supplying, installing, servicing, and maintaining air conditioners. Of all the businesses I ever started, Flat Foot is the only one that survived the test of time. I loved this business and devoted my life to it.

The Eastern Cape Province in South Africa is very rural, has a high level of unemployment, and most of the population lives on less than one dollar a day. These terrible conditions encouraged me to begin a mechanical business that would contribute to employment and, thus, improve the lives of the people in this region. My aim was also to keep people here. Many residents with technical skills went to other provinces, such as Gauteng and Western Cape, for better job opportunities.

In the process of marketing Flat Foot Engineering, I travelled to various government departments—such as the Department of Health and the Department of Education—and pitched my presentations. Once, after a long day of presenting at various government departments, something told me to go to the Botha Sigcawu building. After clearing security with my company profile and a business card, I wound up at the door to the Deeds Office. I politely told the security guard that I worked for a company called Flat Foot and needed to speak to someone regarding air conditioner installation.

He called the manager for me, and within five minutes, a smiling woman opened the door and said, "You came at the right time. I need a quote to install five air conditioners."

I went home to do some math and submitted the quote the following day. Two weeks later, my quote was accepted, and I was instructed to fetch the order and install air conditioners for the Deeds Office in Mthatha. I was so excited to have my first official job!

I needed five air conditioners, but with no money with which to purchase them, I asked my friend Mlungisi John from Port Elizabeth for a loan. He was the one who encouraged and motivated me to start my business and promised to assist me when I did. After explaining my situation, he agreed to buy the air conditioners for a small fee. With no car at the time and only a wheelbarrow, I had to transport the units from my flat in Mthatha to the installation sites. I continued to do the installations myself until I was able to employ a technician, one whose services V & A very generously loaned to me.

I had just finished my first professional installation. I was ready for more and submitted new bids often. Most of those bids weren't selected, but I never gave up.

My break came when I was awarded a project for the South African Post Office to install air conditioners in the Transkei area branches. I immediately started looking for the best suppliers with the best price and service and eventually settled on Border Air Conditioning in East London.

Why Flat Foot?

The name Flat Foot stems from my days as a boxer, where the term is widely used to refer to an unbalanced boxer who does not stand on his toes, or the balls of his feet and is, therefore, easier to knock over. In the early 1990s, when my gym lacked leadership, my teammates and I decided to form a boxing gym called Power Punch. I was a professional boxer at that time and usually assumed the position of trainer.

"Don't be flat-footed!" I would shout at the young boxers. They needed to stay on their toes, so they could move around with more agility in the ring. I said this so much that the young boxers ended up calling me "Flat Foot."

Later in life, my friend Sparks and I used this term often in Mthatha, and it became widely known. The people associated me with the phrase, and the name stuck—everyone in Mthatha and East London knew me as Flat Foot.

"Here comes Flat Foot!" people would shout when they saw me coming in my Alaska-blue Toyota Corolla. The colour of my company logo was inspired by the blue of that car.

It's rewarding that I was able to change the term *flat foot* to be seen in a positive light and that it has become a phrase that is loved by all the people who hear it. In my neighbourhood, people now call themselves Flat Foot with a smile on their faces.

Flat Foot's Early Years

Getting Flat Foot off the ground was not easy. It took time and a lot of effort before I was doing well in my business and enjoyed being a businessman. While I had absolutely no business plan,

I certainly enjoyed running my own business. But I was in no way prepared for tough times.

During the early days of Flat Foot, my life and business were not stressful. In fact, I had no physical signs of stress. I was physically fine and energetic, good looking and fit—if I do say so myself. I was able to travel around the province marketing Flat Foot to potential clients.

I also got involved at a boxing gym in Mthatha called Kwezi Boxing Club. It was run out of a classroom in a public school and managed by Mayaya, as we used to call him. I went to the gym after work and helped train the young boxers. Unfortunately, Kwezi had to close its doors due to a lack of training facilities, plus the school was not keen on allowing us to continue to use the facility. The club later joined Ngangelizwe boxing gym.

I really enjoyed this gym, training and producing good-quality boxers, including Simphiwe Khonco, the International Boxing Organisation's (IBO) world mini-flyweight champion, and Siphamandla Baleni, the former South African champion. I was a role model to them, giving them advice about being a disciplined boxer. But I was also inspired by them and their dreams of greatness.

As with boxing, discipline is the most important skill to possess if you want to run a successful business. Discipline coupled with a clear mission, vision, and purpose are the most essential characteristics for success.

❋ ❋ ❋

In the beginning, even though my company was small, I had enough money for myself. I had financial freedom, but I maintained no clear distinction between Flat Foot money and my personal money. I didn't pay myself a salary; I just used the Flat Foot money as my own. I purchased anything I needed using business money for personal things. To me, that was financial freedom. In my small and ignorant mind, I believed I had made it.

Without a doubt, this was a very bad business practice. In my mind, I was not suffering, and there was no one I had to report to. I was in control of my bank account. I did not know any better then and thought that what I was doing was right . . . until I was declared insolvent in 2013 and had to seek help.

I learned the hard way to separate personal money from business money and to avoid unplanned purchases of unnecessary things. In 2013, I had bought three Volkswagen Amaroks and ten vans. This increased my monthly overhead by 60 percent—something I couldn't afford.

* * *

Business is about building relationships with people, and good relationships are key to the survival of any business. I was very fortunate to have supportive family, friends, and colleagues. My beautiful wife, Vanessa, supports me in every way. Support from your spouse or partner is so important when running a business. I also learned that respect is the ticket to success. Respect is earned, and when you give it, you will automatically receive it.

My mental clarity and stability played a huge role in not only getting Flat Foot off the ground but also making it into the successful business it is today. My boxing training and spiritual support provided by my church are responsible for this. It takes a strong mind and spirit to deal with disappointments like losing out on contracts, missing paperwork, or even people who are intent on seeing your business fail. There are people out there who intend to frustrate or even destroy you and your business. Some will even go out of their way to say things about you, whether to your face or behind your back, and that will discourage you. You must remain strong and never be distracted by such naysayers. Focus instead on your goals.

You can't control what happens to you, but what you *can* control is how you react to such events. You believe in yourself, go the distance, press on, and never give up.

Learning the Trade

I always call myself a self-taught engineer. When I started Flat Foot, I knew nothing about mechanical engineering because I had never gone to a formal school for mechanical engineering. I decided to go to Original Equipment Manufacturers (OEMs) to learn how certain equipment was being manufactured and how it operates. I thought that if I knew how it worked, I could fix it.

I started learning to troubleshoot online by watching videos on compressor windings, installation, gauge use, and all other things related to air conditioners. I then went for courses on high temperature sterilizing equipment and qualified as an accredited installer and maintenance technician. After that, I took a course on industrial laundry equipment and became an accredited installer and maintenance technician. I even did a course on DVM designs through Samsung.

I had no option but to learn the trade. At some point, I would have to talk to my technicians about what they were doing or even go to the work site and do repairs myself. I got so good that I could help a client's maintenance staff sort out a problem with an autoclave by simply speaking to him over the phone about faults and which cycles were not occurring.

TENDERING OFFERS

Tendering an offer is critical to the success of your business. It affects your revenue, cash flow, and profit, so be sure you know how to evaluate all the variables and make the best pricing decisions.

Understanding the Tender Document

Invest as much time as you need to study all the relevant documents, so you can price exactly what the client needs. Be sure you fully understand the requirements, legalities, finances, and the entire scope of the project. This will be an enormous help when it comes time to calculate the correct pricing. Ensure that you have sufficient capacity and qualifications/experience to execute the project to the predetermined standards. It is a disgrace to be awarded a contract only to then discover you cannot perform as expected because you do not have the necessary skills or capital to perform the work.

When you work out your cost for any project, make sure you have the necessary suppliers in place and brief them on the timeline. Being let down by a supplier who cannot fulfill their obligations is another disgrace—one that can cost you and your business a great deal of money.

In order to win, you need to be aware of how your competitors price their jobs. This allows you to rank better in terms of pricing, so you can secure more work. A good practice is to analyse all the tender results and evaluate yourself against your competitors.

Flat Foot goes to all tender openings for any tenders we submit. We record prices, so we can analyse them and base our pricing and strategy accordingly. It also shows that we mean business. Plus, we get to meet some of the individuals involved in the various tenders face-to-face. It is always good to know who you are dealing with and to take advantage of good networking opportunities.

Pricing

Incorrect pricing can be the downfall of any business. When pricing a project, never sell yourself short. You must ensure that all your costs—including labour, overhead, and escalations—are included in your rates and that you can make a comfortable profit. Otherwise, you will very likely lose money—or even worse, your business.

The biggest mistake of my life was when I priced a coal tender for one of the Government Departments. We were caught off-guard when the fuel price skyrocketed during 2017 and 2018. The rand-dollar exchange rate affected the price of fuel and, therefore, affected the coal price. The Department refused to review the tender again to allow for any escalation.

To keep from suffering any more loss, we decided to resign from the project. Our mistake was on the escalation aspect in the tender. We sold ourselves short, allowing less in terms of possible cost escalation.

The lesson here? Never sell yourself short. From that point forward, we always priced with a comfortable margin for potential escalation. Businesses must be sustainable, and there is no sustainability if there is no profit. Like a boxer, you must say *no* to any fights that are not worth your while. Occasionally, boxers do not care about this or how much they are getting paid as long as they are offered a fight. This can be very dangerous because they could be severely injured and might never fight again. Just like a boxer, you need to choose your fights and tenders/projects very carefully, only taking on what you know you can handle and projects that will give you an adequate profit. Otherwise, your business might be knocked out cold, leaving you and your staff either destitute or in a very difficult position.

End of 2017, Flat Foot created a tendering department because we saw the importance of pricing correctly. The staff in this department has been trained to procure the best prices and is tasked with submitting winnable, profitable tenders. Our purchasing policy dictates that we ask for three quotes and choose the one that is best priced. We make sure to study costs and the scope of the work to be provided to be sure that the project is worth our time and that we will reap a profit. By not tendering for projects for which we are likely to carry a loss, our tendering department has made huge strides in ensuring that every project we tender for is one that will benefit the company.

Risk

Managing risk is never an easy task due to the many unknown variables that surround all major business decisions. It is highly critical that an in-depth risk assessment be embedded in the standard policies and procedures of any project plan. Mapping out the probabilities and the subsequent consequences of the project outcome are evaluated to quantify the degree of risk.

Once this is done, action plans are then drawn up to monitor and mitigate these risks. At times, company policies may have to be amended to accommodate a project-specific risk profile. I have found it particularly important to document project risk because it may prove useful in evaluating future projects of a similar nature.

Drawing up project plans prior to the beginning of any project allows for proper resource allocation and material procurement. I make it a point to explain how tender allowances are drawn up and to ensure that daily costing reports are completed on all job sites.

The tender department monitors project performance based on weekly reports. Every month, site agents report on their project costs, and we try to identify areas that could be improved to increase profit margins. It's also important to monitor the effect of interest on long-term loans and to adopt the correct principles of borrowing monies and the implications of an over-investment in fixed assets. I have gained a great understanding of searching for investment opportunities that will maximise profits and reward shareholders.

The scope of all projects should be clearly defined at the beginning, with systems in place so that if the scope changes, project variations are well documented and authorised by the relevant stakeholders before any work is carried out. I go over cost, time, and any additional resources that may be needed with the client prior to the work being carried out. This ensures all projects will be carried out within the budget and the stipulated time period.

There is a tendency in many companies, especially SMMEs, to approach tendering opportunities uniformly across the board instead of evaluating each tender based on the company structure and composition (i.e., resource ability). This should be avoided. Each tender requires a unique approach for which tailor-made strategies are essential.

Changing Strategies

A boxer typically enters a fight with a certain strategy. For example, his approach may have been to fight from the outside and keep moving using his legs, with the aim of tiring out his opponent. But the corner man sees that the opponent keeps landing hard punches. The boxer needs to change his strategy to fight from the inside and bring the fight to the opponent.

In business, it is sometimes important to change your strategy when the initial plan is not working. Your pricing strategy can and will be different from one job to the next. For example, for you to be more competitive, you might mark up your work by 10 percent instead of 15 percent. You may not earn as much profit, but you are better able to compete in terms of price when it comes to tenders and quotes, so you have greater chances of securing the work.

It is essential to calculate the amount of labour needed to be sold every month to cover overhead costs and break even as a business. This gives you a specific target to aim for. For example, Flat Foot sells labour at a certain cost, and if we do not sell any labour, we lose money. Regarding profit, money made is largely derived from the mark-up of the spares we provide in the process.

Business Capacity

After tendering an offer for a big project, a certain client called us in for price negotiations. My mentor and my operations director attended the meeting with me.

The client said, "We are concerned about your capacity to implement this project. On all your tenders, you might have to overlap your staff and use same teams in different projects."

That was true, and I nodded in agreement.

He asked how many staff members worked for me, and I told him I had sixty employees.

"From our point of view, we don't think you have the capacity to run this project. What is your take?" he asked me.

I explained that Flat Foot had the capacity to tackle huge projects in our grade as prescribed by the government, and we could grow our business even further. We had the skills, systems, and infrastructure. We could hire more people if we needed to and could quickly and seamlessly integrate them into our ways. We had a system approach to our business that was ISO9001:2015 certified. Our systems had been audited by external auditors and found to meet the international standards of doing business. We had no doubt that we could complete this service with flying colours.

We were given the opportunity, and we grabbed it with both hands.

A business colleague once asked me if staff complement was the only way to evaluate the capacity of a business. My answer was simple: staff complement *cannot* be the *only* tool used to gauge the capacity of a business. Staff is an overhead that needs to be serviced—the teams you need to engage depend on the availability of work. Revenue guides how many site staff and office staff you should employ.

If you only look at staff complement, you may never know the capacity of the company at face value. Ask the following questions about a company to get your answer:

- Does the company have systems in place?
- Does the company have infrastructure in place?

- Can this company reduce its size when situations dictate?
- Can this company grow without delay when a need arises?
- Does this company have dynamic, experienced, and pragmatic leadership?
- Does this company have access to money?
- Does this company have qualified and experienced staff in their field of service?
- Does the company have a strong administrative support staff?

If the answer to the above questions is yes, you can have confidence that this company has the capacity to tackle any kind of work in their field.

GROWTH

To grow your business, you must have some carefully planned strategies in place for the growth to be manageable. Growth comes with its own challenges, which is why you need to plan and employ the right strategies to deal with business expansion. Growth is most certainly good, but it can be a nightmare if not planned properly.

To progress from an amateur boxer to a professional to a champion, a careful strategy must be in place. One of the most successful boxing trainers in our country, Mzimasi Mnguni, or Bro Mzi, as we affectionately called him, once told me, "Max, when you have the interest of your boxer at heart, you need to carefully plan his development."

Bro Mzi steered the career of world-renowned boxers Welcome Ncita and Vuyani Bungu until they became South African champions, and then he steered them even further to becoming famous IBF world champions. He coached these two boxers and strategically planned their growth by choosing the right opponents for them until they could fight the best in their divisions.

The boxing fraternity in South Africa used to complain that Mr. Mnguni gave his fighters easy victories. His answer to that was, "You need to boost the confidence of your boxer and let him have a couple of victories under his belt. Then when he is ready, give him the tough ones. The chances of winning are greater because the confidence level will be high." The same applies to business: start with smaller projects or jobs you are sure you can handle, and then when you are ready, go for the big ones.

When you have matured enough as a boxer, you are able to handle defeat very differently. You can more easily accept it and then go back and correct the mistakes to improve going forward. In the same way, when your business has developed some muscle through experience and the processes that have been put in place, you are able to better handle any losses and correct mistakes more easily.

In my case, it became very difficult to handle the losses that were caused by a bloated staff complement, which very nearly put an end to my business. Drawing on my boxing experience, I was able to handle defeat and return to the drawing board to correct the issues. When Flat Foot was technically insolvent, I knew there was a way to turn it around. I knew my mistake, and I knew how to correct it. I went back to the basics and drew up a proper business plan, cutting down on my overheads and workload with cash flows and budgets.

Not having a strategy in place when building a champion can be catastrophic. Unfortunately, I didn't select my strategy carefully when growing Flat Foot in the early stages, and I wasn't ready mentally or financially to grow the company. Simply put, there was no strategy in place; we went straight for the kill. Lack of planning was my biggest mistake and one that almost cost me my business.

I saw in my boxing days how young boxers were given the wrong fights in the early stages of their career, only to end up not being the champions they could have been, sometimes getting badly hurt and never fighting again. In other cases, some boxers wanted to fight difficult fights because they thought they were ready, only to be defeated and see their dreams shattered. Experience counts but so does mental and physical readiness. Physical and mental readiness build over time through a clear vision and strategy, and this process can't be rushed.

FLAT FOOT PRODUCTION SYSTEM

In the beginning, we worked without a production system and had no project management system in place. Therefore, we could not monitor any of our technicians, which meant we couldn't monitor costs. Equally important, we were unable to track the company vehicles.

Over time, we developed the Flat Foot Production System. Creating this system allowed us to keep better tabs on the business, and it was paperless. For example, all our technicians use an app on their mobile phones that help the business track calls from the time they are logged until their completion. Tracking calls through the app allows us to see everything that transpired in each specific call, including all costs, profits, and losses.

Below is graphic representation of our production system that took us years to perfect. Perhaps this is something you could implement in your company to achieve efficiency and make a profit.

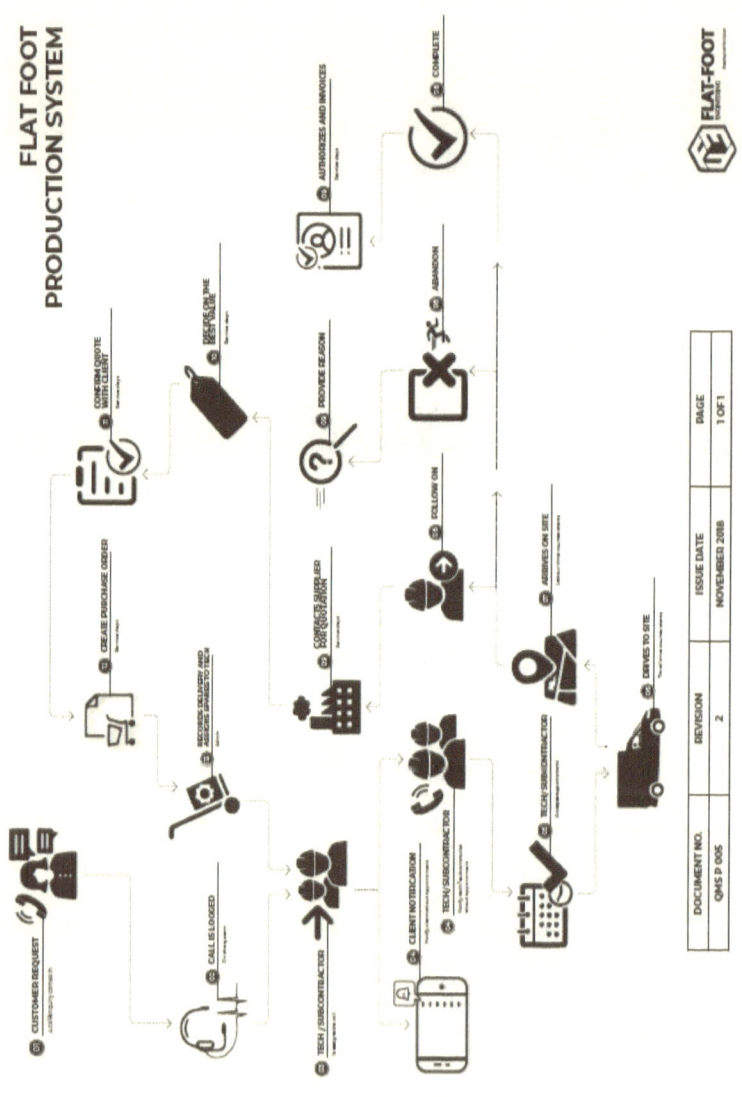

At Flat Foot Engineering, we have a call centre at our head office in East London. Here's how our production system works:

1. An inquiry comes into the call centre via email or telephone call.
2. The service administrator logs the call.
3. The call is assigned to a technician or a subcontractor. The call will appear on the technician's cellphone or tablet, and the technician accepts the call.
4. The service administrator creates an appointment for the technician to go to the job site for an assessment, then notifies the technician and the customer.
5. The technician accepts the appointment.
6. The technician proceeds to the site. He clicks a button that says, "on route to site." Our production system calculates the hours and distance to site.
7. The technician arrives on-site and clicks a button that says, "on site." This will start the clock to calculate the time he spends on-site, so we can invoice the client for the exact time he was there.
8. The technician assesses what needs to be done and captures that information on his phone or tablet, which syncs with our production system. Or he may find that the problem is something that he can fix using the stock we have in the van. He follows the specific protocols that are in the client's service level agreement. When the problem is fixed, the technician clicks "complete" and signs off the job on the system. If more needs to be done on the job and the parts aren't in the van, the technician clicks "follow on." The service department will receive a notification that this technician is working on job number j0001 and needs other parts to complete his work. The service department will contact three

suppliers for quotes. In some cases, such as when the client cancels the job, the technician will click "abandon the job."

9. Our service department assesses and compiles the paperwork for costing and invoicing, then sends the paperwork to the client for payment.

10. When the three quotes for extra parts are received, the service department—in consultation with management—decides which quote to accept.

11. The quote to complete the job is prepared for customer approval.

12. Once approved by the customer, a purchase order is generated for the chosen supplier to deliver the parts.

13. Our administrative staff records the delivered goods, and the service administrator allocates the goods to the technician. Step 3 commences again, and the process is followed until the job is complete.

CASH FLOW

Being awarded a bigger project can be overwhelming for a small-to-medium-sized business owner who is used to running small projects. Very often, the way in which they operate is not geared for long-term growth and sustainability. It becomes a challenge for some entrepreneurs to embrace the change required in their operations when it comes to larger projects, especially regarding new, formal work processes.

For example, when you are considering engaging your firm in a new venture, you need to make sure that everyone understands the scope of the project and that you have the necessary buy-in from your team, including your implementation staff. Otherwise, any so-called newfound growth could be inadvertently mismanaged and subsequently short-lived.

Running a business is like a twelve-round title fight, which requires stamina to go the distance. Stamina is crucial in running a successful business. Growth must be directed slowly for you to endure during the early stages of your venture. You need to be prepared and train hard, and you need to learn from your mentor and take your growth slowly.

Much like the children's story of the tortoise and the hare, it may take you longer to reach your goal, but you will be far more likely to achieve it. Honestly, in business, things very seldom progress as fast as we may like. It takes time to make money by building a business. It is a long road for which planning, stamina, and patient persistence are key.

Furthermore, business is about integrity, honesty, and hard work. Shortcuts and wanting to get rich overnight will not help you. History has proven that those who buy favours to succeed in business have very often been forced to close and frequently end up in prison or facing hefty fines. Such favours are generally short-lived and are not sustainable, besides being downright wrong and falling outside of the law. In South Africa especially, this underhandedness—otherwise known as corruption—is bringing our nation to its knees, which is another consequence that business owners need to take into consideration before taking any shortcuts at the expense of other businesses or our country in general.

Instead, offering a professional service and conducting clean business is the way to go. It also helps to understand that growing a business is a journey with both ups and downs and very little smooth sailing, especially in the early years. You must not be discouraged.

I started Flat Foot in 2006, and it was only in 2019 that we saw some profit. Prior to this, we focused on building the foundation and the walls, and only now are we building the roof so that we can enjoy the benefits of all our work and bask in the satisfaction of a job well done. Not that this means there won't be any more challenges, but at least we are prepared and in a far better position to navigate the inevitable hurdles that will come our way. We are ready for the next leg of our journey.

I have a feeling it's going to be a good one.

Cash Flow Challenges

But in the beginning, I ran Flat Foot like a headless chicken. I had no clue how to manage cash flow. I had no insight and no idea how to deal with things until they ultimately went horribly wrong. In 2013, Flat Foot experienced sudden growth that happened almost overnight. We employed many people and paid them huge salaries with no idea about where the money would come from. As a result, we were declared technically insolvent because we could not pay our creditors. To top it all off, our debtors were not paying us on time. I had to go back to the drawing board and devise a different strategy.

Regarding debtors, the challenge in South Africa pertains to poor payment terms. Our major client is the government, which is consistently very late when it comes to paying for work that has been completed.

When clients do not pay on time, you need to have strategies in place so your business can survive. This can only be achieved through regular cash flow meetings, whereby your cash flow projections are accurately analysed and recorded. Such meetings are a must in any business. You must be able to see who is paying you what and when. This will then assist you in making well-informed decisions. A proper cash flow system helps you to see and plan for the future and predict what will happen in the next few months.

At Flat Foot, we prepare weekly cash flows that also plan for three months in advance, and we use a revenue forecast in conjunction with the cash flow to make decisions and to provide us with targets and goals. We, therefore, know very clearly what we are working toward on a weekly and monthly basis.

Another crucial thing to know is that cash purchases can easily cripple your cash flow. While cash may be king, paying with cash as a small business can diminish your cash flow and even put a stop to it completely. It is best to negotiate sixty to ninety-day accounts whenever it is possible.

Flat Foot clients, especially the government, generally pay us between sixty and ninety days after the final invoice. In such situations, it is vital to have credit terms that can assist you with such unscrupulous and protracted payment terms. I say unscrupulous because overhead costs are paid in thirty days, and if it takes sixty or ninety days to get paid, survival becomes a challenge. The government is fully aware of this but does nothing to rectify the problem. After all, killing a small business is very easy: give them work, then delay the payments to them. In South Africa, many businesses are out of work today not because they do not know what they are doing or offer a shoddy service, but because they are forced to liquidate due to payment delays that almost appear carefully planned to frustrate and destroy the entrepreneurs of our country. What is so frustrating is that the policies are in place to pay suppliers within thirty days, but after twenty years of doing business with the government, I am sorry to say this is not the case. There is always some long story, a missing order or wrong allocation, or just no money with which to pay. It is costing businesses their lifeblood and, with that, the employment they provide. It very nearly cost Flat Foot our business.

Being a small business owner is stressful because if anything goes wrong, you have much to lose. We put our hearts and souls in these businesses in the hopes of making money and creating job opportunities, but you then find yourself being stressed about everything. You're stressed about getting work, and then once you do get it, you're even more stressed about getting paid. Late payment of suppliers is a thorny issue, and I am convinced that it is not getting the attention it deserves at the official level.

While politicians are talking about thirty-day payments, government departments are doing the opposite. This discrepancy is a serious issue with severe consequences. For the sake of the many businesses that are very negatively impacted by this, our government must ramp up its efforts to rectify this. Change must start with the officials who are ultimately responsible for ensuring that all payments are made on time.

One principle you must know in business is that your creditors are your business partners, and once you understand this truth, you will never go wrong. So, pay your creditors on time and be open with them. Communicate with them and make them understand whatever problems you might be experiencing, especially when it comes to delayed payments. You are far more likely to receive a sympathetic ear and retain their support if you clearly communicate with them. Also, once you promise something, stick to your promise and walk the talk. A broken promise leads to broken trust, and trust is key in any business relationship, no more so than when it comes to finance and creditors.

We manage our creditors very carefully at Flat Foot, and our policy is not to have anything sitting on ninety and one hundred and twenty days on our creditors' age analysis. We always strive to stick to our credit terms, which has reaped huge dividends as far as securing credit is concerned.

Just like a boxer who uses his jab to keep his opponent at bay, the following are some of the tactics I have used in running Flat Foot to our immense benefit:

1. Early payment discounts. From time to time, we ask our clients to pay early if they can in return for a discount on their invoices. This strategy has helped us greatly, and we frequently get paid within only seven days for a 5 percent discount. This will differ from client to client, some of whom receive a 2.5 percent discount for payment within thirty days.

2. Invoice discount. This type of transaction is normally done by banks and will give you about 80 percent of the value of your invoices owed to you by your customers upfront, though terms and conditions apply. However, invoice discounts tend to be problematic if your order book is based on government contracts alone.

3. Bank overdraft. A bank overdraft can assist your business with cash flow in days of need whilst waiting for payment from customers. Interest is payable on any overdraft amount, hence we only use this as a backup when we really need to.

4. Eastern Cape Development Cooperation Jobs Fund. This initiative of the Eastern Cape Government through the Eastern Cape Development Cooperation (ECDC) pays a struggling company ZAR 10,000 per job to retain jobs in our country. This fund assisted us for at least one month to ensure that our staff salaries were paid at a time when we were struggling financially.

In addition to the above, Flat Foot has also implemented a debtors-creditors mirroring mechanism, which ensures payments released to suppliers are timed in a manner that minimises releasing funds the company has not yet received. In addition, we always strive to avoid making purchases towards the month's end to extend dates for amounts due as far as possible to allow for sufficient time for debt collection. It is also important that the company negotiates sixty to ninety-day payment terms with its creditors, as we have noticed recently that government and private entities have been delaying payments. It is also important to ensure that the company has a sufficient private client split in its debtor's book so as not to rely only on government work, which slows down during elections and yearly budgets.

Collections of payments owed are crucial in your business. The squeaky wheel indeed gets the grease. If you do not follow up on your monies, you will never get paid on time. At Flat Foot, we hold weekly debtors' meetings where we create service and finance reports on collections of monies. If we are owed any money, we make sure that the client hears from us almost every day, especially for poor-paying customers. Our service department will elevate the report to management if they are battling to acquire payments from our customers. Once a debt has reached ninety days, we write a letter of demand. Then we hand it over to the lawyers when they hit one hundred and twenty days or more. To safeguard us from non-paying clients, we now ask new customers for a 50 percent deposit upfront and the other 50 percent upon completion.

If our projects and cash flow had been managed properly in our early years, Flat Foot would have made money as opposed to losing it. Changing our culture and way of doing things, holding monthly management meetings and weekly cash flow meetings, and now having introduced our app-based Flat Foot production system have all greatly improved our efficiency and profitability.

CUTTING COSTS

The best way to keep your finger on the pulse of your company's financials is to conduct regular management meetings where you discuss management accounts (overheads, cost of sales, and direct/indirect labour) and cash flow. You should also calculate a revenue forecast to help plan for your targets and where the revenue will come from. It is very important to be 99.9 percent sure where the revenue will come from at least three months in advance. If you can't forecast that far out, you need to reduce your overheads because cash flow will kill you, and you will experience a loss.

Remember, overhead costs differ for different companies. Flat Foot overheads are different from other companies, hence the different rates that we use to charge our customers. Calculate your cost properly before accepting client rates. You can't negotiate rates with potential customers if you don't know the actual cost of running your team.

Salaries

Salaries are the major cost in any business. At Flat Foot, we need to sell at least one hundred and forty hours per month per team for us to break even. We pay technicians for eight hours a day, so we expect them to sell those eight hours, or at least sell an average of six hours a day. Our rates are calculated by considering the cost of a team with a van. There are a lot of variables that you must look at when pricing for your team.

Below is an email I had to send out when Flat Foot needed to cut costs:

Hi Team,

In the past couple of months, we have realised that the company is under financial distress because our major client, which is Government, has for the longest time reduced our flow of work. In order to make sure that we do not strain the finances of the business, we decided to do the following:

Decreased time for technicians.

Management, including Keith and Ravi, took a 10 percent cut in their salary.

We have realised that the site costs are managed better through decreased time for technicians, but our overheads remained the same. As a result, we've been experiencing a loss. The reality is that our overheads are geared for a two to three million turnover per month, and currently we are battling to turn even ZAR 1.2 million a month. This isn't anyone's fault. It's the circumstances we find ourselves in.

As management, we needed to safeguard the business, and we appreciate the reality that if we don't reduce our overheads immediately, we won't have a business to run. Our overheads are higher than our revenue. In business, that's a recipe for disaster. Now that we've looked at the business in its entirety, we came to the conclusion that cutting costs is the only solution to turn the business around.

Having said all the above, it's not all dark—there is some good news. We are finalising the discussions with one of the Government Departments regarding our appointment on the submitted tenders. This tender will enable us to invoice approximately two million a month, which will be an acceptable ratio as far as revenue and overheads are concerned.

My assumption is that the belt tightening will be for only two months, namely June and July. As I see it, the appointment will come at the end of June, and July will be for all the compliance and signing of the contracts. The real work will start in August.

In view of all the above facts, management agreed to implement the following, of course with your buy-in as an important stakeholder:

- I (Max) will take a further 10 percent reduction in salary.
- Ravi has agreed to forfeit his salary for the period while we are under strain.
- Admin staff will have to rotate (Ravi has some suggestions, but we need to discuss them as a team so there's buy-in from you guys).
- Keith will come down on Monday, so he can be part of the discussions.

In conclusion, I'm confident that this belt tightening will be for a short period of approximately two months, and then things will go back to normal.

We have not forgotten that salaries have remained the same for a while now, and we are convinced that we'll be able to look at them once we get these appointments. These appointments will guarantee us revenue for two years, and that will enable us to plan things better when we have recurring revenue.

Regards,
Max Mabuti

And here is the email I sent my staff after I realized I would not be able to pay their salaries. I strive to always be open and honest with my staff.

Dear Team,

On behalf of the company, I apologize for the expected delay in payment of full salaries. We know this creates financial distress or strain for everyone. We are expecting a payment from one of our clients to be made on 5th June, to clear on 7th June. Decisions to mitigate the situation have been made, and unfortunately, salaries have been affected.

Regrettably, we will only be able to pay part of your salaries on 31st May. The outstanding amounts will be paid by 7th June, worst case. I say worst case scenario because Pragma (SASOL) might come to our rescue as indicated earlier this week.

I must state my concern about government always dropping the ball when it comes to paying small businesses. We are at the mercy of government officials to do the right thing and pay small businesses on time. I can only hope for the best.

We are humbly apologetic for the inconvenience and the delayed notification on such a sensitive issue.

Regards,
Max Mabuti

We weren't in this situation because we couldn't manage our cash flow. We suffered because the government delayed our payments.

COMPLIANCE

My friend Donavan Smith once said, "Max, sometimes you need to be a *cowboy* when you run a business."

Flat Foot had tendered for a project with the municipality in Port Elizabeth. One of the requirements was that we needed to have an office in the metro. I received a call from Nelson Mandela Bay informing me that for us to be considered for the job, they needed to come to my office to carry out an inspection. At the time, we had no office in Port Elizabeth. And yet, my answer was simple: "I will give you directions to my office in the morning."

I put the phone down and thought of Donovan's advice that in business, you must sometimes be a cowboy. I immediately called my cousin, David Loff, who also worked for Flat Foot.

"David, I am coming to Port Elizabeth," I said. "We need to open an office there tonight because tomorrow there's to be an inspection."

I hung up, jumped in my car, and arrived in Port Elizabeth around 3 p.m. Whilst on the road, I made a few phone calls to some property agents and was lucky enough to find an office that was available at Newton Park, a good location.

I called David again. "Cuz, where are you? Can you meet me in town?"

Within a few minutes, my cousin was there, and we deliberated on how we could furnish this new place to be as professional as possible. David told me about a friend who used to have an office in Bluewater Bay and would, hopefully, still have all the furniture. Lady Luck smiled upon us again. His friend not only had all the furniture but also was willing to sell it to us. We agreed on a price and went to collect everything. By the early hours of the next morning, we had furnished the office.

As promised, the people from Nelson Mandela Bay arrived and were ultimately satisfied with their office visit. Even though we were not successful with the tender, this marked the beginning of having a branch office in Port Elizabeth. Strategically, this was a great move because it placed us firmly in the Eastern Cape and gave us a strong geographic presence, allowing us to tackle jobs from all over the province.

I recall the words of Richard Branson: "When you are asked to get involved in an opportunity you are not sure you want to be involved in, say YES and learn to do it later." Because I said YES and set up an office in less than a day, our Port Elizabeth office is still in operation.

The Road to Compliance

In the early days of Flat Foot, even though we always respected the law and attempted to comply with the various legislations, we never made it a business priority. That all changed when I could not obtain a tax clearance to apply for financial assistance from the Small Enterprise Finance Agency (SEDA). SEDA was established in 2012 because of the merger of South African Micro Apex Fund, Khula Enterprise Finance Ltd., and the small business activities of IDC. This organisation funds small businesses up to ZAR five million.

As required by law, South African Revenue Services (SARS) auditors randomly select tax periods for selected companies for an audit. Flat Foot was audited in 2016, and SARS wanted to see our records from January 2013 up to and including July 2015. We needed to be ready to cooperate with them and provide all necessary information to their satisfaction. This posed a serious challenge, as it tested the company's professionalism regarding document retention and filing. Ultimately unable to provide the auditors with everything they needed, this resulted in the disallowance of some claimed expenditures and led to a SARS debt, penalties, and interests.

As prescribed by South African law, you cannot trade with the state when you are not compliant with the state laws, especially tax laws. Treasury regulations require valid tax clearance for any bid or request for quotation from any state enterprise, government department, or municipality. It was a major blow for Flat Foot to be rendered non-operational, especially since most of our business came from government departments in the Eastern Cape province.

We had no choice but to go to SARS and negotiate payment terms (Deferral Payment Arrangement, or DPA). The DPA assisted in unlocking the trading part of the compliance requirements, but it came with a major strain on our cashflow. Any delay in paying the agreed amount would lead to the immediate forfeiture of the agreement, and the entire debt would be instantly reinstated. It was a precarious situation, one we had to delicately maneuver as we struggled to survive this trying period.

If your business is predominantly public sector-oriented, compliance must be your top priority. Business opportunities and getting paid will hinge upon this cornerstone, and it deems you a reputable and dependable business.

I am, however, appalled by the behaviour of some SARS officials when it comes to small businesses in South Africa. The South African president has encouraged entrepreneurs to work together with the government to create much-needed jobs and reduce the high unemployment rate that has haunted our nation since the dawn of its democracy.

President Ramaphosa has described the unemployment rate of 29 percent in South Africa as a "deep and serious crisis." Whilst small businesses have tirelessly taken up the challenge to battle unemployment, some SARS officials are making it hard or downright impossible for small businesses to operate, using tax laws to frustrate the business owners. Some business owners are only too quick to close shop. Oftentimes, the implementation of tax laws depends upon who you are and the colour of your skin. SARS officials do not listen to the facts that contribute to a business being unable to pay a SARS debt (i.e., they knowingly block your company from the central supplier database [SCD], so you won't get paid).

It's a vicious cycle. If you aren't getting paid by the government for services rendered, you cannot pay the government to which you owe money. They prefer that you close your business. This is a direct contradiction to what President Cyril Ramaphosa is preaching. Audit officials are no longer doing their job but using their status to deal with personal vendettas and settling scores. For example, simply because you lost an invoice from an old period they are auditing, they disallow clear transactions in your bank, even though you are paying a reputable supplier. Furthermore, they levy a 150 percent penalty. They can issue such a hefty penalty that you will essentially be working for SARS for the rest of your life. This is not fair.

These officials have the power to destroy good businesses that are contributing to the growth and wealth of our country, and they must be stopped.

Use an Accounting Firm

Choosing the right professional accounting firm as your SARS representative is very important. I made the mistake of not looking into the firm I used, and their unprofessionalism is what led to my troubles with SARS. This accountant was very popular in construction circles, and because of this, I trusted their judgement and never questioned any of their submissions to SARS. As long as I received my tax clearance, I thought everything was fine.

When I found out how risky and reckless they were being by taking shortcuts and failing to do things properly, I ultimately fired them. Previously, we had employed a bookkeeper but decided it would be far better to use the services of an accounting company. We ultimately hired a new, extremely professional company that would do things right and not take any shortcuts. We also decided to acquire a better accounting system. It was critical to build the necessary capacity in our small accounting department to ensure that we never again experienced problems with SARS and that the business remained compliant.

Flat Foot makes it a point to budget for all compliance fees, and we pay our Value-added Tax (VAT) to SARS every month. We also make sure that our Pay as You Earn (PAYE) and Unemployment Insurance Fund (UIF) contributions are paid before the seventh of each month.

Even though conditions are somewhat unfavourable for entrepreneurs to survive and succeed, compliance should always be at the forefront of a business owner's mind. In South Africa, in particular, if you want to do business with the government, you must comply with all legal and Receiver of Revenue obligations.

Compliance with the laws that govern business in your country is critical to the success of your business. You don't want to find yourself on the wrong side of the law by taking chances or doing things incorrectly or even illegally. Be above-board and upfront in all your business dealings.

9

INSOLVENCY

In 2013, Flat Foot underwent some very rapid growth. We had just been appointed by Sasol, Ltd.[2] to carry out preventative maintenance of all their filling stations in the Eastern Cape.

Sean Khosa from SASOL told me, "I see you, Max, employing more than one hundred employees in the next five years. I see the commitment and hunger in your eyes."

Almost overnight, we grew to sixty staff members and bought far too many vehicles. This move made our overheads sky-high, and suddenly, we were unable to handle both our projects and our labour. Then Flat Foot, the business I had

---

[2]   Sasol Limited is an international integrated chemicals and energy company that develops and commercializes technologies and builds and operates facilities to produce a range of product streams, including liquid fuels, chemicals, and low-carbon electricity.

started and spent so much time and energy on, was declared technically insolvent.

At the time, I owed money to my suppliers, my staff, and the Receiver of Revenue (SARS). On top of that, the bank that had loaned money for my business was considering a liquidation process for Flat Foot. To make matters *even* worse, SARS wanted to lay criminal charges against me because I hadn't paid my staff Pay As You Earn (PAYE) contributions. Accordingly, most of my staff were by now on a go-slow (they came to work but were non-productive), having referred my case to the Department of Labour who, in turn, demanded that I pay them the money I owed. As for the department officials, they couldn't care less that I was getting paid by the Government Department, which was partly to blame for the predicament I was in.

"We are not responsible if you receive payments from your clients," they said. All they wanted was the outstanding money.

Because of all this, most of my staff members left, some of whom sent letters to lawyers who demanded their money. All my creditors wanted their monies as well, and the high court sheriffs were daily visitors to my office. This all made for a very financially difficult situation, the culmination of which finally brought Flat Foot to its knees.

Instead of accepting defeat and throwing in the towel, I took total responsibility for everything. The insolvency happened because I had not invested enough attention in my business, particularly the financial side. I had trusted my management too much. We only occasionally discussed business strategy, and I blindly accepted their ideas and suggestions without doing my own research. I was leading from behind and not taking charge of the situation.

So, I went back to my boxing techniques and used the strategies I had learned there: take an eight-count and then return to my corner to come up with a new plan of attack. I needed to be honest with all my creditors, including my staff, and I developed payment plans for everyone.

Breaking Point

At some point in my life as a businessman, I opened a recording company, which I called Flat Foot Records. Some of the artists I produced include Super, Double Dose, Jigga, Mzobhana, and DJ Tulz. I had a distribution deal with a company called Revolver in Durban, South Africa. I met Zwesta in Mthatha in 2012 through a friend who wanted to produce an album with him, and I soon decided I wanted him to be a producer for my artists too. He was staying at a place called Ngangelizwe in Mthatha at the time, and I saw talent in this young lad.

I wanted him to record my artists at that time, but my recording company couldn't carry the overhead of his salary, so I offered him a job at Flat Foot. During his spare time, he agreed to help me with Flat Foot recording tasks. However, Flat Foot Records fell victim to cash flow constraints, and I had to close down the company. I asked Zwesta to stay with me in the apartment where Flat Foot had started. I employed him as a receptionist for three months, then promoted him to technician, then later to a company accountant.

I desperately needed funds to turn Flat Foot around—about $320,000 (ZAR 5 million), to be precise. There were times when I wanted to give up, but as a young boxer, I never gave up any of my fights. I always made sure that I went the distance. I knew I couldn't give up my Flat Foot dream. I decided to tell my staff and the people who had stood by my side that I would give them an early warning to look for other jobs if ever the time came when I knew I couldn't revive the company. This was only fair to them, even though it was the last thing I ever wanted to do.

There were times when I wanted to give up. But the voice of my boxing trainer, Ta Mengo, kept popping into my mind: "I see your opponent is getting tired. I saw his eyes—you are about to finish him off. You are behind on points, but don't give up. Move around and try to tire him out, and then throw the right punch, which is the punch he does not see."

Moving forward, Zwesta was now that voice.

"Don't give up, Bro Max," he whispered in his soft voice.

I am forever grateful for having Zwesta by my side. He pledged to walk this road with me and stand by my side.

"Bro Max," Zwesta shouted one morning, as they normally call me at work. "Are you giving up? You can't, not now," he said.

"Let's do this," I said. I could not give up my dream of building a business that would one day operate without me—and which I could eventually sell.

We went back to the basics. We decided to look for someone to help us prepare a business plan, only to discover that it would cost us almost two thousand dollars (ZAR 30,000), money we did not have. So, we decided to prepare our own business plan and immediately got to work on the first draft. This gave me the opportunity to finally know my business—my target market and my overheads—better.

Whilst we were working on the plan, the business had to continue, and we made sure our clients were not affected by this insolvency. We travelled around to ask people to invest in Flat Foot, even travelling as far as Johannesburg to see if we could source an investor, but nothing ever came of it.

Then, a few weeks later, my friends Lwanda Figlan and Don Smith introduced me to Ravi Moodley. I met with him at a bar in East London and told him my story. He believed in me and said to bring him a business plan with cash flows and a revenue forecast the following day at his office. I immediately called Zwesta, and we went straight to the Flat Foot office to prepare.

We were at Umso Construction's offices in Beacon Bay at nine o'clock the next morning. Ravi saw how committed we were to turning things around, and he also saw a future for our business. After listening to our presentation, he was so impressed that he invited his partners, Tollo Nkosi and Peter Jung, to invest money in our business. The agreement was that they would invest the money, and the money they invested would, in turn, "buy" them shares of stock. But I also had to pay them back with interest over time. It was a tough negotiation because Flat Foot was technically insolvent. I gave them each 20 percent stock, and I retained 40 percent. It was my only option to save my company, and I had to take it.

This lifeline was the turning point in Flat Foot's trajectory.

DANGER: HAVING ONLY ONE CUSTOMER

When we joined the Top 40 National Gazelles, Flat Foot was introduced to the Business Doctors, who in turn introduced us to The Value Builder System, a methodology to improve the value of your company. John Warrillow, its founder, refers to his Value Builder Drivers as the Switzerland Structure, a name inspired by Switzerland's focus on neutrality.

This programme came just as Flat Foot was looking for help to turn our business around. One of the value drivers we focused on was the risk of having one customer.

Having only one customer is risky because if anything bad happens to that relationship, or your customer goes under or cannot pay, your business can suffer to the extent that you may have to close your doors. Recurring revenue is at the very heart of business survival. You, therefore, require contracts that will guarantee revenue on an ongoing basis.

Flat Foot had only one customer in our early days. Unfortunately, that customer was our poor-paying government—90 percent of our revenue came from Government. Our business model was centred on the planned maintenance programme of medical facilities. As a company, our management team made a business decision to mitigate this risk. We adopted the following approach:

- Diversify our order book
- Get private clients in our order book
- Allow no single customer to contribute more than 50 percent of our revenue by the end of 2019. Reduce that number to 20 percent going forward.
- Obtain a national footprint by 2019

This strategy helped us sustain our business, especially when our contract with the Government came to an end—an end that was unfortunately not communicated in a timely manner for any planning. Basically, we were caught by surprise. Government stopped allocating work to us, and if we hadn't mitigated that risk, we would have closed our doors. Fortunately, we had worked very hard the previous year to build our name and market our business in Johannesburg. Through that marketing—and thanks to our national operations manager—we managed to obtain new clients in the Gauteng region, which helped keep Flat Foot afloat.

By using The Value Builder System, we started to increase the value of our business. We focused on all The Value Builder drivers and evaluated our business using the system's tools. They gave us a technical analogy with which to augment our strategy in building our business. To know more about the value builder system, read John Warrillow's *Built to Sell: Creating a Business*

That Can Thrive Without You. This book will give you all the information you need to build the value of your business.

We have since greatly diversified our customer base, which now includes both private and government clients. We will not fall into the same trap again—and neither should you.

THE VALUE OF A MENTOR

When Flat Foot was technically insolvent, I had to look for help. Just like in boxing, you need a corner man or a trainer in business. A corner man is an additional force or set of brains behind the boxer, providing advice or support when it is needed most. This person also acts as additional protection for the boxer because sometimes the boxer might think he is winning, but the corner man can see exactly how the fight is progressing and that it might require a change of tactics. Sometimes, for instance, the corner man may throw in the towel to stop the fight so that the boxer doesn't get too badly injured or never fight again. Every entrepreneur or business owner needs a mentor to help steer their business to success.

After putting some feelers out, I was introduced to a fine businessman named Ravi Moodley, who had a wealth of experience in construction. I approached him to mentor me.

In boxing, a corner man is essentially there to help you to win the fight. This person can see your mistakes objectively and correct them, as well as see your opponent's mistakes and their strong points. They advise you accordingly. When you are too close to the fight, it becomes difficult to see your mistakes or even your strengths. The corner man may sometimes appear to be harsh when offering advice, but it is advice that is necessary. The same applies in business. A mentor can look at your business objectively and guide you to success.

Ravi Moodley was very strict. He made it a rule that we hold regular management meetings and prepare reports for our shareholders and that we also hold weekly cash flow meetings. Ravi's mentorship boosted my esteem as a business owner and instilled in me and my business a culture of accountability and honesty.

It is important to note that when you agree to be mentored, you must also be willing to be led. Remember, a mentor is someone who has done it all before and is, therefore, wiser and more experienced, so you need to listen to what he or she tells you and, most importantly, act accordingly. Even if the advice given may appear harsh or contrary to what you might have in mind, you must always look at the bigger picture, which is the success of your business. You must be willing to be told what to do and comply. Being able to *act* on what you have been told or advised to do is *critical*.

Of course, there are times when my mentor and I disagree. After a meeting, I might feel like telling him where to get off, but Ravi's advice always leads me in the right direction. Like a boxer, you need to undergo a prolonged and rigorous training programme with a reputable trainer to be fit to take on any opponent. Similarly, mentorship can take years of training, communication, critique, and advice to bear fruit. You will become better every day through mentorship.

Because of Ravi's guidance, Flat Foot has not only survived and thrived, but we have won many awards. In 2013, Flat Foot achieved the status of professionalism, our quality management system was certified, and we achieved an ISO9001:2008 status, which was recently upgraded to ISO9001:2015. Our initial ISO9001:2008 status was sponsored by Turner & Townsend (a global consultancy business serving clients in the real estate, infrastructure, and natural resources sectors) as part of their enterprise development commitment. They employed consultants to assist us in achieving the status. This was also part of SASOL giving back to the community, having requested Turner & Townsend to cover the certification costs to redress the imbalances of the past in South Africa. We have maintained our ISO9001:2015 status to this day.

In 2016, we were chosen as one of the Top 40 National Gazelles, a prestigious status in our country of high-growth small businesses, which in turn led the government to believe that our company would generate more employment and contribute to the South African National Development Plan 2030. This plan seeks to create eleven million jobs, 90 percent of which should come directly from small businesses. In 2017, we won silver in the prestigious ROCCI/FNB Business of the Year Awards and then went on to win the Oliver Top Empowerment 2018 Awards. Flat Foot has more than stood the test of time. While other businesses have been unable to survive the current recession, we have sustained our business throughout these tough times.

I am so grateful that Ravi Moodley gave his time and talents to mentor me and never gave up on me. My debt to him can never be repaid.

For small businesses to succeed, they must have a mentor on their payroll. I say payroll because if you are paying for something, you will respect it and make the necessary time for it. Mentorship is money well spent and could mean the difference between failing or succeeding in your venture. This makes mentorship priceless.

I was raised by parents who taught me the values of *Ubuntu,* an African idiom meaning "humanity," and of giving a helping hand. I am always willing to share the help I was given by my mentor with other small business owners. Writing this book is a way of giving back and motivating struggling business owners.

JOB DESCRIPTIONS

Job descriptions communicate the expectations that come with every position. Correct job descriptions are also critical in supporting almost every employment action, including recruitment, performance management, training and development, compensation, recognition and rewards, promotion, discipline, and termination.

While job descriptions are not legally required, they certainly serve as essential business practice for both the company and the employees. It is of utmost importance that everyone knows very clearly what is expected of them and why. This is what Geoff Green called "purposes" in his book *The Smart Business Exit*. Without a fully defined purpose, employees can't know what is ultimately expected of them.

A business owner can use a good job description not only as a valuable aid in the job-recruiting process but also as an outline for reporting relationships and working conditions. A well-crafted job description can also be used for:

- Performance Management: Set measurable performance goals based on duties in the job description. Coach employees to meet these goals.
- Training and Development: Provide information about promotions, classes, seminars, and other career development activities.
- Compensation: Clearly outline the compensation programme with minimums and maximums for each position.
- Recognition and Rewards: Act as a baseline for performance but also include tools on how to perform above and beyond what is asked.
- Discipline: Illustrate what will happen if an employee does not adequately perform their respective job functions.
- Return-to-Work Programmes: Prepare light or modified duty options to facilitate a smooth transition from occupational injury or leave.

At Flat Foot, we want to do everything in our power to build the capacity of our staff. This commitment has been made and documented in our ISO2009;2015 quality management systems. Our engineering staff, for example, is regularly sent to training courses, some of which are conducted by the manufacturers of the equipment we use. This helps our technical staff to be one step ahead of the competition and to keep abreast of the technology currently used in the market.

The journey from our conventional way of doing things to going paperless has not been easy. It requires a change of culture. The older generation is very resistant to change and prefers to stick with the status quo. To help them acclimate, we held workshops for all technical teams, so they could see the benefits of technology in our industry. The fourth industrial revolution is real, and Flat Foot has already started to prepare for the future. "Stepping into the Future" is our slogan, and we want to be leaders in technological advancement.

At Flat Foot, our staff is the very heartbeat of our business. We invest in our staff and are always open with them. They are aware of when the company is doing well and are also informed when the company is under pressure. And when times are tough, I lead from the front. And when things are going well, I work behind the scenes and allow my staff to take the lead and be recognised for their initiative.

STAFF SELECTION

In my opinion, the correct utilisation of staff is vital to any business. You can probably price correctly in your quote and see if you are making a profit and covering all your overheads, but if your operations are not carefully monitored, you are in danger of losing a lot of money.

You need to select your team very carefully, choosing people who will easily fit into the culture of your business. Failure to do so can lead to all sorts of problems. Without your team fully on your side and prepared to do the work that is expected of them, not only will your business suffer, but the rotten apple syndrome could affect the productivity of the rest of your staff.

To be successful as a boxer, your team is of vital importance. The same principle applies in business.

At one point, Flat Foot employed people who we thought were good, but we failed to check if they conformed to our culture. Ultimately, we had to let these staff members go. Today, our human resources department makes sure the people we employ fully understand and share the same culture and values as our business.

Employment Equity

In South Africa, employment equity is both necessary and important in our country's attempt to redress the wrongs of the past. During apartheid, black people were marginalised in society and in the workplace, deemed inferior, and paid less than their white counterparts. To undo this legacy, post-1994 employers are now compelled by law to ensure that all people are treated equally and afforded the same opportunities in terms of employment and promotion.

Flat Foot has taken it upon ourselves to adopt an employment equity policy whereby all people are remunerated equally. It does not matter whether you are black, yellow, white, or pink—your salary is based on your expertise, qualifications, and the position you hold. We not only believe in equal job opportunities, but we believe that we are all equal as humans and deserve the same recognition and rewards. This has paid huge dividends for our company, as our staff is motivated to always perform at their best, knowing that they will be rewarded because of it.

Flat Foot advocates for integrity and ethics. I run a professional organisation with equally professional staff. We provide professional advice to our clients and execute projects professionally and with integrity. We pride ourselves on the way we do business, and we always go above and beyond the clients' expectations.

I agree with Vusi Thembekwayo, a South African motivational speaker and entrepreneur who said, "If you do your work and you achieve your targets, and your output makes sense to the business, it does not matter whether you work from home or at the restaurant. As long as you meet your deadlines and you are creative, I am happy."

PROFESSIONAL DEVELOPMENT

Many business owners fear that if they train their staff, they will leave with their newfound skills and look for better opportunities—or even start a competing company. In business, there will always be some level of risk in whatever you do, risk you can never entirely eliminate. Therefore, if you want to succeed, you need to trust your staff. The real question is this: What if you train your staff and they stay?

Do not be afraid to train your staff with the necessary skills. After all, you are paying your employees to do their job, so it is up to you to give them the tools and necessary skills they need to excel. Send them offsite to train and provide them with on-the-job training.

Your staff is essential to keeping your business open, running smoothly, and successful. You need them to help you move your business forward.

In South Africa, our government encourages staff training and development and provides incentives to train your staff through the Sector Education and Training Authority (SETA), which was established to help implement the National Skills Development Strategy to increase people's skills in their respective sectors. Flat Foot belongs to SETA, and the government is helping us to up-skill our staff members with grant funding. For your business to benefit from this funding, you must first register with SETA and be compliant with business governing regulations to qualify for the grant.

At Flat Foot, regular staff training is integral to our business, for which we have a skills matrix that is reviewed every six months. As with any business, employees can prove to be challenging. Like the ones who can be trained and show potential but display no interest in the training programmes. I call these people dead wood, and they have no place in a company. It's a hard decision to let any employee go, but if it's for the good of the company, then you must let them go.

At one point, we rented a house in Port Elizabeth to accommodate staff when they carried out jobs in the area. One day, my cousin, David Loff, visited the house and immediately called me, saying, "Cuz, you will not believe what I have seen here. Your trusted comrade is running a company within your company, and I have the company registration documents in my hand." Apparently, this trusted comrade was using me and my resources to build his empire.

I was understandably shocked by this news and had to confront him. When I did so, he never denied it and had no option but to resign. This taught me to employ people who share the same culture and vision. The culture at Flat Foot is based on honesty and integrity, but the people I employed in those early days were dishonest and only out to serve themselves. They were stealing from me. It was a very bitter pill to swallow, but it also taught me that trust must be earned rather than merely assumed. This lesson has paid dividends ever since, as the current Flat Foot staff members are wonderful, and I trust them implicitly. You can have all the right contracts and contacts, but trust is the most important principle in business.

To assist Flat Foot with all labour issues, including training and development, we have employed the services of a human resource consultant from a company called LabourNet. This has paid huge dividends for our company while saving us a lot of money and time in the process.

It is essential that you regularly review your company policies and weigh them against actual measured objectives. You may need to alter policies from time to time based on the prevailing climate and circumstances, but most important is that you have a clear and concise policy in place that guides both your business and employees. It can make all the difference when the going gets tough, which is par for the course for any business, especially during the growth phase.

Internal Communication

Regular communication with your staff is essential. Failure to communicate in a timely manner and in a clear and respectful tone limits your employees' ability to do their jobs effectively, which inevitably disrupts operations. It is of fundamental importance that you establish an effective internal communication system whereby problems can be identified and rectified speedily, changes to strategy can be discussed and implemented, and communication can easily flow between departments and between managers and lower-level employees. This also helps to build staff morale, as they will feel included in the decision-making processes that affect both the business and themselves.

External Communication

External communication is easily hindered by a small business's inability to employ the necessary staff to speak to clients and other businesses. There is no simpler way of losing business than poor communication. Even if all you can afford is a half-day secretary, for instance, who can take care of this aspect of the business, it will be worth it in the long run.

FINDING AND TRAINING YOUR REPLACEMENT

The benefit of you training your replacement is that you get to transfer your skills and share your knowledge with the younger generation. You get to see new talent and excited young blood take your business to the next level. This also gives you the bonus of being able to take time off. You have a valuable business if your business can operate without you.

I do not work late anymore because we have the right people in the right places, and the business can operate without me. My replacement can take care of everything for me. This leaves me with more time for my family and to travel the world. I can see what is going on at work no matter where in the world I am by logging in to the system. This is what I call freedom.

In business, you get to a stage where you find yourself unnecessary. This is what John Warrillow, in his book *Build to Sell*, refers to as "spoke" and "hub." You must never be the spoke and hub of your business. You must always strive to make sure your business is not centred on you.

I was scared to train my replacement until I realised that Flat Foot would have no value if everything relied on me. We developed a clear succession plan, and I am training my replacement to run the business the best way possible and even better. Songezo and I go to meetings together, and I introduce him to all my clients and business peers. He represents our business on all international business missions sponsored by the government. When presenting Flat Foot, I would introduce the business to the potential customer and give background on who we are, our culture, our strategy, and our future. Songezo would then explain how we are achieving our goals and unpacking the Flat Foot production system.

I believe in Miles Monroe's[3] theory that leadership is like running a relay—you need to pass it on. The trick is not how you run but how you pass the baton to the next person. You should train your replacement and let him run your business whilst you are there so that you can mentor him.

In 2012, I became a boxing promoter to nurture talented boxers in the professional ranks and ensure they succeed in life. I trained these boxers in my style of boxing, taught them the type of training and diet I followed when I was a boxer, and showed them tricks to lose weight to fight in the correct

---

[3]   Miles Monroe was a Bahamian evangelist and ordained minister and an avid professor of the Kingdom of God. He was an author, speaker, and leadership consultant who founded and led the Bahamas Faith Ministries. In his book *Passing It On,* he speaks about growing future leaders.

division. Mentoring young boxers is no easy task. It requires strength and commitment from both sides.

It is possible that your mission was to start the business and build the foundation and hand it over to someone whose mission is to take it to higher levels and build your legacy. Remember that in relay running, you pass the baton to the next person, and we all become winners.

Zola, a business leader who owned a construction company, told me that he didn't believe in training his replacement; he only trusted himself in his business. He said they wouldn't do things right, and he'd end up doing them himself. Why should he train them when he doesn't trust them?

I asked him, "What will happen to your business when you are sick, let alone dying? Who will continue your legacy? Who will service your customers when you are unable to? What happens when you want to go on leave?"

He was unable to give me a straight answer.

I said, "My brother, what happens if you don't train them, and they stay with you? That's when they become a liability."

Training your replacement should never be ignored. Don't take your skills with you when you die. The greatest leaders are those who find their replacements, train them, and let them do it on their own.

My Replacement Resigns

When Songezo resigned from Flat Foot in 2019, it was a painful loss to the business and to me. It was like my dreams were being destroyed.

"I think my time here has come to an end, Bro Max," he told me on that fateful day. "I would like to resign due to growth. I feel I have done my part as mandated by you when you appointed me. I want to pursue another direction in my life, and I have taken a long time thinking about my decision. I believe I am doing the right thing."

I replied, "Songezo, even though it is sad to let you go, I am convinced that you have thought about what you are doing very carefully. Who am I to keep you from your dreams? You have my blessing. Go and make me proud. I know you will do great."

Though I had seen it coming a few months back, I was still shocked. Songezo was training the staff to know what he did for the company and mentoring them to step in for him should they need to. He was a leader. He never wanted to leave a vacuum in the company; he wanted to ensure that work continued as usual whether he was there or not.

Songezo joined us with a mission to accomplish, and he did just that. His contributions left us with a user-friendly system that allows the business to run smoothly. It is going to be a huge task to fill his shoes, one that will take time. Finding your replacement is not an easy job, but if your strategy is to build a business that could survive without you, then you have no option but to continue looking for your replacement.

LEAVING A LEGACY

When I started Flat Foot, I never wanted to be a stumbling block to the company's growth. I knew from the start that, at some point, I would need partners to help me take this business to the next level. Sometimes God provides people with mandates, and mine was to create Flat Foot and then enlist the help of others to make that dream a reality.

Finding my partners was a journey in and of itself. I cannot say that I was entirely ready to take on partners at this stage, but circumstances left me with no choice but to do so. Looking back, I am very thankful for those circumstances because I no longer take all the risks and make all the decisions alone. Whoever runs the business needs to report monthly to all partners so that together the team can ensure the business is running properly and without negligence. Such a business will have a far greater chance of surviving than a company controlled by a single individual. To me, this is a huge plus.

Though I was obviously emotionally attached to Flat Foot—passion, after all, is emotion—I was mindful of the fact that if I wanted this dream to succeed, I needed people who could help me. I was prepared to share this pie with other like-minded entrepreneurs and work together as a team to keep it afloat and moving forward. I now have some great partners I can rely on. Remember that when you have partners, there is accountability. The chances of making poor decisions that could be detrimental to your business are minimised because you must consult with someone else before acting.

The Flat Foot team and I now believe that my mandate is to build Flat Foot to the level of a global player in the mechanical industry. At some point, I believe I will be a co-owner of a multinational company turning over billions of Rands. We still have a lot of work to do, but we are getting there.

I once told Sbali, a friend of mine who owns a construction business based in East London, that it was high time he got partners in his business. He was very dismissive of my idea, saying he liked things the way they were—he ran the show, *Yishow yam*. In Xhosa, this means that he controls everything.

I told him that having more than one head pushing to achieve a goal is better than a single head. Consulting with others before making decisions is critical in business. I reminded him that having help would take his business to the next level.

Lend a Helping Hand

Giving back to the community is one of my passions. Flat Foot has assisted numerous small construction companies and developed them by giving them work and helping to increase their Construction Industry Development Board (CIDB) grade. The CIDB grades companies based on their experience and capacity, and this grade is very important if you want to do business with the state.

We also support a small non-governmental organisation called Community Action Africa (CAA), which helps young schoolchildren focus on math and science, encourages them to study, and assists them in doing so. We have committed ourselves to assisting in this noble cause.

And recently Flat Foot Engineering has been involved in helping the Guardians of Hope (a home for abandoned babies) to renovate their new home in East London.

MAKING THE DIFFICULT DECISIONS

When I was first getting started, I was unable to make difficult decisions when I needed to, which cost me a lot of money. The company overheads were high, and there was no income. When I realised I was in danger—when no work was forthcoming—I wanted to hold on to my staff and not lay them off. I was worried about them and didn't want to contribute to the unemployment rate. I couldn't afford my team, but I also couldn't afford to let them go. This was bad for business and my employees, who were not receiving an income.

Difficult decisions also come when an employee needs to be fired. Sometimes when your company grows, people have trouble adapting to the new culture. I call these people right-wingers, people who like the status quo and don't want to change. Sometimes you need to make a difficult decision and get rid of the dead wood.

When a major client of ours delayed the appointment of contractors due to the company's database experiencing problems, Flat Foot was adversely impacted. At this time, I failed to make a difficult decision. I was worried about my staff, so I kept them on even though I could no longer afford them.

If you are honest with yourself about the state of things, it will likely take you much longer to build your business, but you will sleep peacefully at night. There are no shortcuts to building a business. There are times when you need to do what must be done and deal with the consequences later.

In South Africa, the buzzword is corruption, which is very real and killing our economy. They say power corrupts, and in our country, we are faced with a situation whereby our leaders—both in government and in business—are unable to handle the power that has been entrusted to them. I have learned that you need to be humble and respect your clients and your employees, for which honesty and integrity are key. Respect goes a long way, and respect is earned.

I have also learned that you must never forget where you came from, and you must always remember those who have helped you climb the ladder of success because you might need them if ever you fall back down. The experience I have accrued over the years has made me wiser and a lot more careful when making decisions. I now consult with experts and people wiser than me. Remaining humble is key to running a business, no matter how successful. Arrogance merely turns people against you. Take responsibility for your actions, say thank you, and acknowledge people's contributions to your life and business.

Since 2017, we've grown Flat Foot by 30 percent each financial year. Even though we have mastered the financial management aspect of the business, every decision we make is based on our financial performance, and we sometimes still have to make difficult decisions every now and then to keep the company going.

Remember to be open and honest with your team and get them involved in decision-making, especially when it involves their livelihood. At Flat Foot, it was the employees themselves who suggested they be placed on unpaid leave when I was unable to pay their salaries. This is a sure sign everyone at Flat Foot has a common goal and is actively working toward it.

In South Africa, most start-ups fail in the first one thousand days because they are afraid or too despondent to press on. When difficult times pop up, and they always do, go back to the basics of your business, employ the necessary strategies to extricate yourself from whatever predicament you are facing, and, most importantly, get yourself a suitable and trusted corner man. This makes your chances of winning the fight very high.

TRAVELLING THE WORLD

M any of my trips to countries around the world have been funded by the government, specifically the Small Enterprise Development Agency and the Department of Trade and Industry. They selected Flat Foot to represent South Africa in a number of trade missions to showcase to the world what South Africa has to offer as a nation and as business people. The mission of our government is to attract investments to our country by ensuring that manufacturing is taking place inside our shores to service the world, boost our economy, and create needed jobs in our country.

South Korea

I took my first trip overseas in June of 2017—a trip to South Korea sponsored by Samsung. I remember the Monday morning when I received the news that I'd be going. The clouds had a tint of orange, and the breeze was nice and cool; I could feel deep down that something good was coming.

A tall, well-dressed middle-aged man arrived at my East London office. His name was Joseph Kaseke, a Samsung sales engineer, and he said, "Max, I am sending you to Korea for being one of Samsung's dealers that is doing very well in your area of jurisdiction. Samsung has committed to supporting you."

As you can well imagine, I was very excited by this news, much like a child given toys on Christmas Day. Samsung was paying for everything, including airfare, accommodations, and food for the seven-day educational trip to their head office.

The day of the trip finally arrived. Having never travelled on a plane for more than five hours, this was going to be interesting. I decided to pack only a small bag to travel, leaving sufficient room to spoil myself with souvenirs and do some clothes shopping. (Little did I know then that Koreans are smaller people compared to the average person in South Africa, so I never got any clothes.) We travelled in style with Emirates Airlines via Dubai and then met up with colleagues from other African states when we arrived in South Korea. It was the best time of my life as we were touring Samsung, learning about its history and its future. We were also taken to the future museum of Samsung products that will hopefully be launched soon.

I met the vice president of Samsung and most of the decision-makers in the company. This was a huge eye-opener for me, and it helped prepare me to look for bigger things to come my way.

China

Out of the blue one day, I received an application form from the Small Enterprise Development Agency to accompany the South African Minister of Small Business Development on a government trip to Guangzhou, China. I filled it out and submitted it right away—I couldn't let an opportunity like this pass me by. After some time, I received an email that said my application had been selected. I was very excited to represent my country in China and showcase what Flat Foot had to offer in the engineering space. I was amongst a group of entrepreneurs from all over South Africa who were chosen to represent their respective companies at the South African small business fraternity at the 14th Annual China International Small and Medium Enterprise Fair (CISMEF). This trip was very important for South Africa as a member of the BRICS nations.[4]

Flat Foot was now playing in the international arena. When we arrived in China, we were transported to a hotel, and the next day we were taken to the conference centre for the exhibition. With South African flags in our hands, we went straight to our stand. South Africa was one of the hosts of the event, and our stand was full of people taking pictures. The South African setup was a huge attraction, and we couldn't hold our excitement as we took pictures to post on social media and to send to our families.

We spent four days in China, rubbing shoulders with like-minded businesspeople from around the world. This was a real revelation to me, as I got to have first-hand experience of how the Chinese were doing business. This visit also exposed Flat Foot to an international audience.

---

[4]   BRICS is an acronym coined for an association of five major emerging national economies: Brazil, Russia, India, China, and South Africa. Originally the first four were grouped as BRIC—before the induction of South Africa in 2010. It was a big deal for South Africa to become a member of the emerging economies; hence, China became an important trading partner for South Africa.

Las Vegas

My third trip overseas was to Las Vegas, Nevada, USA, in February 2018. This trip was again made possible by SEDA, but this time was in conjunction with The Value Builder System's owner John Warrillow. I was invited by The Value Builder System to give a speech during The Value Builder Summit.

What touched me most was when SEDA said that I would not be going there alone. I would be accompanied by the manager of SEDA, Duma Maqubela, along with Dali Mjekula, a SEDA business consultant. I was also very humbled to see the CEO of Mthiya Dynamics, Mr. Zukile Nomafu, the gentleman who introduced me to The Value Builder System. We arrived in Las Vegas on 30 January 2018, and Mr. Nomafu joined us on 2 February at Las Vegas's Caesars Palace.

When the time came for me to make my presentation, people in the audience shed some tears as I narrated my story of how we survived being declared insolvent, owing to numerous creditors, and the bank filing for liquidation, to becoming a company that won many prestigious awards and was regarded as a National Gazelle, a company that helped our government curb unemployment in South Africa.

Afterward, I was interviewed by John Warrillow, who asked, "Against all odds and coming from a poor family, you became one of the most respected businessmen in the world. How did you do that?"

"It's because I used my experience as a young boxer and never wanted to give up my dream, just like I never gave up as a young fighter," I answered.

This was my first time visiting the United States. Las Vegas had long been one of the cities I had wanted to visit due to its huge boxing history, and I loved every moment of it. I took time to visit the Mayweather Boxing Club and was very excited to see the boxing gym of one of the greatest fighters the sport has ever produced. Unfortunately, I did not meet Floyd, but I was happy to see his gym.

Second Trip to China

My second trip to China was again sponsored by SEDA, and it was another opportunity to engage with businesses in the country. This was the 15th Annual China International Small and Medium Enterprise Fair, and I was asked to present Flat Foot to the Chinese delegation for possible business partnerships.

We were all greatly excited about this trip, though what was most exciting was a business meeting with the international boiler manufacturing company, Zhengzhou Boilers. This meeting was arranged by our office to discuss a possible working relationship with Flat Foot. It turned out to be a great success, which led us to look for opportunities in South Africa on the energy side of the boiler industry.

Flat Foot was among the businesses chosen to make a presentation. With the help of an interpreter, my presentation was given in both English and Chinese. It was another eye-opener for me, being in a foreign country presenting with an interpreter of a language you can neither speak nor understand.

India

My trip to India was one of the most exciting trips I have ever taken. The Indian business community shares the same history with South Africa, and the ties between South Africa and India date back to the days of Mahatma Gandhi. The Indian community has an appetite to do business with South Africa, and that has motivated me a lot.

MEDIA RELEASE
DATE: 10 JULY 2019
EASTERN CAPE ENGINEERING COMPANY TO
EXPLORE EXPORT OPPORTUNITIES IN INDIA

The Managing Director of Flat Foot Engineering in East London, Mr. Max Mabuti, says his company is looking forward to exploring export and investment opportunities during an Outward Trade Mission (OTM) to New Delhi and Mumbai, India organised by the Department of Trade and Industry (**the dti**) from 15-19 July 2019.

Flat Foot Engineering is part of the twenty-seven companies that received financial support from **the dti**'s Export Marketing and Investment Assistance Scheme (EMIA) to participate in the mission; to increase trade of value-added goods and services into the Indian market.

Mabuti says he is excited about the opportunity that **the dti** offers him through the mission to travel to India where he is hoping to get investors for his electro-mechanic projects in South Africa. The company, which has branches in Mthatha, Port Elizabeth, and Johannesburg, provides manufacturing and installation of hot water pressure vessels and boiler inline filtration system services.

"Currently, we are trading domestic, and the trip to India presents an opportunity to realise our ambitions of growing our footprint beyond South African borders by expanding our market to other continents, especially in Asia. We will be using the week-long event to network with businesspeople from that side with the hope of finding potential suitors who can be interested in investing in our company," says Mabuti.

Mabuti points out that he is yet to secure trade leads but says he remains optimistic that they will secure some better outcomes that will assist his company to increase production and create more job opportunities. Presently, the firm, which was established in 2006, employs sixty people.

The mission will comprise of a trade and investment seminar, business-to-business meetings, and site visits. Companies that will participate in the mission are operating in the agro-processing, electro-technical, and defence.

During my trip, I obtained some opportunities for a partnership with an Indian company to set up a plant in South Africa that will lead to us employing about two thousand people.

Germany

In 2019, I received an email from the Eastern Cape Development Corporation (ECDC) that informed me of a pilot project sponsored by a partnership between Germany and the South African Department of Trade and Industry. This was a management training programme of the GIZ GmbH, financed by the Federal Ministry for Economic Affairs and Energy (BMWi). The training was from 29 October to 22 November in Cologne, Germany, and was hosted by TÜV Rheinland Academy.

They asked various types of companies to apply to this prestigious programme. The primary focus was to create a platform to encourage German companies to partner with South African small and medium-sized businesses.

I immediately submitted my application, and three weeks later, I received an email stating I was shortlisted for an interview with the German delegation, which would happen in a week's time. I knew that Flat Foot's story of being a hidden champion would help us be selected to go to Germany for the training. I knew Flat Foot would spark someone's interest and make them want to know more about me, my story, and my company.

Two German nationals came to interview me.

One said, "Max, your story is inspiring, and we hope to see you soon."

"I will see you in Germany!" I said while I walked through the corridor where other business colleagues were gathered and had come to be interviewed.

Lilia and Inna, the facilitators of our training, prepared the manager training programme at TÜV Rheinland Academy. This course, which I called a mini-MBA, was very intense, and we learned a lot about running a business and the German culture of doing things.

One of our missions was for each business leader to use his or her skills to find a German partner. I travelled around Germany by train and bus looking for one. I woke up at 5 a.m. to be at the main train station to take the fast train four hours from Cologne to Krefeld to visit the main offices of CERTUSS, a steam boiler manufacturer. I was to meet with Holger Deimann, global sales and marketing director. I arrived a bit early, but Holger was waiting and ready to see me. Ultimately, we signed a dealership agreement, and my mission was accomplished.

My visit to Germany was a success. I passed my course and am convinced that my German partnership will be a long-lasting one. I also met amazing South African business colleagues who all became my friends, and I am grateful that we created a WhatsApp group where we communicate and share ideas.

I am so grateful to the German government for hosting us and to the Eastern Cape Development Corporation and the Department of Trade and Industry for believing in me as a business leader and affording me the opportunity to be amongst the twenty businesses representing South Africa. We were the pilot group, and our success or failure would determine if the partnership between Germany and South Africa continued. We represented our country well, and the next group of businesses will go to Germany and achieve what we did.

These overseas trips have helped me comprehend the world better by showing me how other nations do business. They have also opened opportunities for Flat Foot and South Africans to benefit from the experience and expertise of people all over the world in business and technology. I made the decision to use my skills and the many tips of the trade I gathered to assist my fellow small business colleagues in the Eastern Cape and the rest of South Africa. This is something I continue to do today.

REBRANDING FLAT FOOT

When I started Flat Foot, I needed a logo that would turn heads. After thirteen years in business, it was time for a more corporate look. In 2017, we were chosen as one of the high-growth companies in South Africa to undergo an intense training funded by Hitachi and spearheaded by Thinkroom, a consulting company that specialises in small business support.

Andre Young from Creative Designs came up with a brilliant logo for us that was simple and still included our well-known blue colour theme.

Flat Foot needed a tagline, so I asked George and Songezo for advice. Because foot is in the company's name, I wanted something related to feet, but that would also stand the test of time. We brainstormed many ideas, and George finally came up with "Stepping into the Future."

We will always step into the future with our Flat Foot.

AFTERWORD

Being an entrepreneur is not easy, and I know it's a challenging journey, but you can build a successful business if you persevere, press on, and go the distance. I always tell business owners that spectators are excellent boxers because they are not physically involved in the fight. They see your mistakes and strengths. A corner man's mission is to help you win the fight, and he's busy studying the fight, so he can advise you between rounds before letting you get back in the ring. A mentor does not run the business for you but helps you win. Mentorship is crucial in business.

Tough times are guaranteed in business, but they are not forever. Nothing is permanent in life; even the economy has a cycle. When bad times arrive, press on and don't give up. When good times arrive, you must not be complacent. Don't lose focus because that may cost you the fight in the last round. You need to do things right and be a responsible entrepreneur.

This book has helped me achieve my goal and purpose in life. I want to inspire and motivate struggling business owners to press on and keep up the fight of building sustainable businesses that will create job opportunities and contribute to national economies.

There's nothing wrong with making mistakes. However, mistakes only become an issue if you do not learn from them. I hope this book encourages readers to learn from my mistakes and take on the strategies I used to keep Flat Foot alive and thriving.

ABOUT THE AUTHOR

Max Mabuti began his career as a professional boxer but quickly became a business leader in Mthatha in the Eastern Cape, South Africa. Armed with a wheelbarrow and a dream, Max set out to found a mechanical engineering company, Flat-Foot Engineering, where he is currently the managing director.

Max's particularly unique philosophy is "Business as a Boxing Match." He compares business with a boxing match and all its survival tactics. He believes that, as in boxing, a business owner needs a corner man from whom to solicit advice during every round of the match. A business owner—like a boxer who needs a trainer or corner man—also needs a mentor for continued advice and guidance.

Max and his wife Vanessa have two children, Ethan and Marley. They have another baby on the way.

9 7 8 1 9 5 5 7 1 1 1 1 1